Anatomy of a Vase

Nurcan Candemir

AOS Publishing, 2025

Copyright © 2025

Nurcan Candemir

ISBN: 978-1-998662-99-9

Cover Design: Meredith Lindsay

Visit AOS Publishing's website:
www.aospublishing.com

Dedication

For those who have strived,
fallen, and shattered, and
those who have risen again.

Contents

Introduction

In the vast symphony of existence, we are more than mere beings; we are vessels crafted by the hands of the Divine, designed to engage with the world around us in ways both profound and magnificent. I liken this vessel to a vase; a vase waiting to be filled, waiting to express the essence of who we are. We have been endowed with the capacity for wonder, for connection, and for creation. Each of us is brimming with potential, ready to overflow with the essence of our being and leave an indelible mark on the world.

Imagine yourself as this vase, empty yearning for meaning. You have the power to choose what to pour into it, and those choices will shape your essence. What you fill this vase with will define your journey, your beliefs, your desires, and your intentions for life.

In life, balance is key. They say 'pick your poison' , but I say 'pick your fill' . Pour hot water into a vase, and you'll see it splinter, creating cracks and threatening to explode, spilling its contents all over your living room floor. Similarly, see what happens when you fill a vase with extremely cold water—it fogs up, creating moisture that dampens everything around it, clouding and chilling the contents with it.

Now let's set the liquids aside. What happens when we place something top-heavy into the vase? It topples over, with the potential to spill its contents, creating a mess, and possibly falling and shattering on the floor—a bigger mess still. And what if we put nothing into it at all? It may look pretty for a while on the bench or bookshelf, but if we don't tend to it, it eventually becomes a dust magnet for spiders to nest and dwell in.

Finally, let's imagine we put the right amount of water into it, along with the prettiest assortment of flowers. What happens then? We all enjoy the fragrance and assortment of blooms; they brighten our day and enlighten our spirit. This is our task—to fill our lives with this kind of balance. However, this is not a one-time solution. Even with the right water and flowers, if they are left untended for too long, the water becomes stagnant and green, and the flowers wilt.

Life is about constantly maintaining this balance. The poems contained herein metaphorically begin with the vase and explore our earnest efforts and what we do with our vessel. What we fill our vase with ultimately manifests from the conditions of our heart. Fill your vase with purpose and meaning, with love and joy. This doesn't mean there's no room for sadness and anger, but we shouldn't overdo it, lest we risk the vase shattering.

The Vase of Life

Amid the music of creation, we are hollowed clay,
Moulded by the Infinite to meet life's wild array.
We are vessels—vessels of great, wondrous, and
sometimes dire things,
Interacting, immersing, communicating; life's melody
sings.

Picture, if you will, yourself as this vessel, this sacred vase,
Awaiting life's touch, longing to embrace.
Within this vessel resides the power to choose and decide
What essence to pour, what journey to abide.

We stand as vases, waiting to be filled
By the choices we make, by the paths we build.
Each decision is a stroke upon life's canvas,
Defining our journey, our beliefs, our purpose, our
chances.

At times we stand tall, resolute, and bright,
Basking in the dawn's gentle light.
But life's tempests may come, and we may fall;
Yet we rise again, unbowed, unbroken, standing tall.

Sometimes we topple, we tumble, we roll;
Yet from these falls, we find the depths of our soul.
We may chip, we may crack, but we do not shatter,
For within us lies resilience, character, and matter.

But alas, there are times when life's cruel hand
Shatters us, leaving us broken and scattered across the
land.
We lie in fragments, shattered and torn,
Longing for solace, feeling forlorn.

Yet with the Divine Will, we rise once more,
Gathering our pieces from the floor.
Each shard is a memory, a lesson, a scar,
Each one weaving into the fabric of who we are.

With trembling hands, we mend and bind,
Trying to reclaim what's left behind.
Jagged edges, glued with care,
Creating a vessel more unique, more rare.

But let us not forget, as we traverse this grand gallery,
In our quest for understanding, for love, for clarity.
Let us not be the force that shatters,
For it's not just the vessel, but what truly matters.

For every break, every chip, every scar
Adds depth to our being, both near and far.
So let us be kind, let us be true,
For in this gallery of life, I'm a vessel, and so are you.

Part 1 - The Empty Vase

In the stagnant lull of mid-morning, the house feels heavy with silence. The only sounds I hear are the monotonous ticking of a clock and the occasional, indifferent hum of a passing car. Sunlight filters through dusty blinds, casting lifeless shadows on the worn carpeted floor. A faint breeze slips through a window left slightly ajar, carrying the faint scent of wilting jasmine from the neglected garden outside.

This is a moment of oppressive stillness in a life stage where monotony prevails. The children are at school, the frantic bustle of the morning has given way to a void, and the burdens of the afternoon loom ominously on the horizon. It's a time filled with the emptiness of unfulfilled plans and a cooling cup of coffee, forgotten on the kitchen table (as it so often is), emblematic of fading warmth and interest.

In this stifling silence, there's a pervasive sense of listlessness and ennui. My mind is weighed down—not by pressing tasks, but by the lack of purpose, the void of meaningful engagement. It's a time to stare blankly, to feel the creeping dissatisfaction with the way the light dulls the room, the worn texture of the carpet beneath my feet, the aimless chatter of birds outside.

These moments of drab simplicity often blend together in an unremarkable blur, adding to the sense of life passing by without significance. They are the empty spaces between events, the pauses that highlight a lack of direction. It's a stage where one endures the ordinary, finding it increasingly hard to ignore the nagging sense of discontent and the feeling that something crucial is missing.

Such a time could relate to any phase of life—a retiree grappling with the emptiness of unstructured days, a stay-at-home parent struggling with isolation, the monotony of a couple who've been married for a significant length of time, or someone working from home left disconnected and uninspired. These bleak interludes remind us that life isn't always about grand milestones but also about the wearying, everyday moments that bring a deep, pervasive sense of unease.

A Vacant Display

In the corner it stands, a magnificent sight,
An empty vase gleaming in the light.
Once filled with love, vibrant and bold,
Now it sits empty, its story untold.

A vessel of beauty, now a home for the small
Insects and spiders, who've made their call.
Once filled with dreams, now void and hollow,
A relic of love that couldn't follow.

The luster has faded, the magic is gone;
The once-enchanting beauty feels forlorn.
Its elegance tarnished, its glory now past,
A symbol of love that didn't last.

Oh, how it once shone with such grace.
Now it sits in the corner, out of place.
A symbol of emptiness, a vessel of sorrow,
Forgotten and abandoned, no hope for tomorrow.

Yet in its decay, a story resides
Of love and loss, of forgotten tides.
Though now it's worn and filled with despair,
It once held love, hopes, and care.

So let it stand, though faded and worn,
A testament to the love once sworn.
For even in emptiness, beauty can lie
In the dust-covered corners where memories fly.

The Dispassionate

In the gallery of life, a heart is on display,
Once vibrant and full, now in disarray.
An empty vessel, once brimming with light,
Now shadowed by darkness, lost in the night.

Once adorned with love, a masterpiece divine,
Now a hollow shell where dreams decline.
Its beats, once rhythmic, now echo alone;
In the caverns of emptiness, they're silently thrown.

Sadness gathers around it, settling like regret.
As time passes by, the heart can't forget.
In the corners of memory, shadows find a home,
Feeding on lost hopes where love used to roam.

The sparkle has dulled, the magic has fled,
Leaving behind echoes of words left unsaid.
Once a beacon of joy, now a relic of pain,
A silent witness to love's bitter refrain.

Yet in its emptiness, a story unfolds
Of love lost and battles untold.
Though now it's worn and filled with despair,
It once beat with passion beyond compare.

Longing

Emptiness, a weight I wear—
A hollow feeling, hard to bear.
Despair whispers, "No one's there"
In this vast expanse of lonely air.

Emptiness, a gaping hole,
Where hurt resides, taking its toll.
Depression like a heavy knoll,
Weighing down my wounded soul.

But in the midst of this endless night,
A glimmer of hope, a shining light—
A hand reached out, so pure, so bright,
Bringing warmth to my cold, dark night.

Longing fills the silent night,
A yearning for a guiding light,
To chase away this endless plight
And turn my darkness into sight.

With love and kindness, the emptiness fills
And the heart that once lay cold and still
Now beats with hope, a newfound thrill,
A symphony of life, against despair's shrill.

Loneliness fades as connections grow.
Sadness wanes as love starts to flow.
In the arms of others, I come to know
That even in darkness, there's a chance to grow.

Empty vessels stand,
Once filled with love, now hollow—
Echoes of lost dreams.

Part 2 - The Vase Half Full/Empty

There comes a time in one's life, a delicate stage, when one feels like everything is standing at the edge of a vast, serene lake. It's a moment where the water's surface mirrors one's life, reflecting both the calm and the restlessness that tug at one's heart. For me, this was the mid-career plateau, a time where the glass is half-full and half-empty, a poignant blend of contentment and longing.

On one hand, the glass simmers with gratitude. Years of hard work have paved the way to a stable career, a reliable income, and perhaps a family that fills one with warmth and purpose. A home, no longer just a place to sleep, is a sanctuary filled with personal stories and memories. This stage offers a sense of security, a comfort in the familiar rhythm of daily life.

Yet on the other hand, the glass seems half-empty. The dreams that once ignited one's passion may now flicker softly, overshadowed by routine and predictability. The thrilling ascent of one's early career has levelled out into a plateau, where the horizon feels unchanging, and the summit of one's true potential remains just out of reach. There's a quiet whisper of what-if, a contemplation of roads not taken, dreams delayed, and passions left untouched. Time feels more precious, ticking by with an insistent reminder to rekindle one's purpose and zest for life.

This duality plays out in the fabric of one's everyday moments. There's pride in the work one has accomplished, yet a tinge of restlessness as friends leap into unknown ventures, succeeding in ways that stir one's own dormant aspirations. It's a reflective pause, a time to cherish the fullness of what one has achieved while also acknowledging the emptiness that invites new possibilities. Here, one can choose to savour the view from where one stands or to stir the waters, seeking new reflections and horizons beyond the familiar shore.

The Indeterminant Display

In a room of shadows, there sits a vase
Half-full of sunlight, half-lost in the haze.
A vessel of glass, fragile and true,
Reflecting the world in its watery view.

Half-full, they say, with hope in their eyes,
Seeing the light where darkness lies.
Half-empty, others sigh and concede,
Focusing on what they lack, what they need.

But oh, dear heart, take a moment to see:
The vase holds both in its transparency.
For life, like this vessel, is a curious blend
Of hope and despair, of beginning and end.

In the half that's empty lies room to grow,
To fill with dreams and let them flow.
In the half that's full lies joys to treasure,
Moments of bliss, beyond all measure.

So when life feels heavy, when shadows fall,
Remember the vase, standing tall.
For in its simplicity is a truth we find,
That half empty or full, life is kind.

It's not about what's lost or gained,
But how we see, how we're unchained.
For in every moment, a choice to be
Half-empty, half-full, or simply free.

The Vacillating Soul

In the deep recesses of my chest resides a heart,
A heart that beats with a rhythm of art.
But within its chambers, a tumultuous sea
Of emotions swirling, tumultuously free.

Optimism, a ray of golden light,
Yet shadowed by clouds, within the fight.
Pessimism lurks in corners dark,
Casting doubt, leaving its mark.

Contentment whispers softly, a soothing balm;
Amidst the chaos, a tranquil calm.
Ambivalence dances between hope and despair—
Uncertain, indecisive, lingering in the air.

Determination rises, a flame within,
Seeing potential where others see sin.
The glass may be half-empty, but I see
Opportunity and possibility waiting for me.

Gratitude blooms like a fragrant flower,
For the moments of sunshine, for every hour.
For the half-full glass, for the half-empty, too;
Grateful for the journey, for all that I knew.

My heart, a vessel of indeterminate grace,
Navigating emotions in this human race.
With each beat, a story told
Of optimism, pessimism, and courage bold.

At a Loss for More

In the depths of my chest,
an uncertain heart dwells,
where optimism meets pessimism,
swirling endlessly.
Contentment tries to soothe,
quieten the inner storm,
but ambivalence, like fog,
obscures the form.
Determination whispers softly,
"There's yet room to grow;
though the glass seems half-empty,
there's more to know."
Gratitude, with gentle hands,
tries to ease the ache,
reminding me of blessings
with every step I take.

My heart is a tangled web:
emotions intertwined,
hope and sadness dance
in the corridors of my mind.
Some days the glass is half-full,
some days it's nearly dry;
in this indeterminate state,
I lose the strength to try.
In the space between
uncertainty and clarity,
lies potential for neglect,
a sad new reality.
No determination,
no gratitude by my side,
my heart navigates this journey
with loss as its guide.

Chambered heart beats strong;
Emotions swirl like a song.
Half-full, half-lost.

Part 3 - The Vase of Neglect

In the entirety of life's stages, there exists a shadowed interval where neglect seeps in like a slow, insidious fog. This stage often lurks in the years of mid-adulthood, where the relentless demands of career, family, and societal expectations converge into a cacophony that drowns out the softer, yet vital, needs of self-care and personal connection.

We want to aim for that promotion, but with it comes a heavier burden of responsibility. Days stretch into nights as emails pile up, meetings multiply, and deadlines loom. In this relentless pursuit, physical health begins to falter; the morning runs are skipped, replaced by hurried cups of coffee and quick meals snatched at desks. The body responds with fatigue, weight gain, and a persistent ache that is no longer just metaphorical.

Parallel to this, the emotional bonds that once were the foundation of joy and support begin to fray. Relationships with partners, children, and friends grow strained as time together becomes a luxury rather than a given. Intimate conversations are replaced with logistical discussions—who will pick up the kids, and so forth. The once-vibrant connection with a spouse might now feel like a partnership in routine, rather than a bond of love and companionship.

Hobbies and passions that once brought a spark to life are pushed aside, deemed non-essential in the face of more pressing demands. The guitar gathers dust in the corner, the unfinished novel languishes in a drawer, and the camera, once a portal to capturing beauty, now sits unused. The creative soul, neglected, begins to feel the weight of monotony and routine. Sleep becomes restless, the mind racing with unfinished tasks and future anxieties. The concept of mindfulness and being present in the moment becomes a distant ideal rather than a practiced reality.

In this stage of life, neglect is not a deliberate act of abandonment but rather the byproduct of misplaced priorities and overwhelming pressures. It is a slow drift away from the self, where the urgent continually overshadows the important.

Forsaken

In the corner of the room,
shadows deep,
a vase sits silently
where none care to peep.

Once-vibrant blooms
are now withered, forlorn,
mourning in the stillness
of neglect.

Stagnant waters, sickly green,
reflect neglect,
the passage of rue.
Mouldy whispers
cling to frail petals.

Forgotten tale,
despair sets sail.

Once they danced
in the sun's warm embrace,
now trapped in a cycle
time cannot erase.

Their fragrance tainted,
a foul, musty scent;
in this realm of neglect,
they lament.

Each petal droops,
a silent plea
for a touch of care,
a chance to be free.

Alas, they wilt
in solitude's grasp.
In neglectful silence,
they gasp.

Mould creeps like ivy,
its scent filling the air;
a bouquet of neglect,
a sight so unfair.

Once a proud bouquet,
now a pitiful sight
left to wither and fade
in dimming light.

The vase, once cherished,
now abandoned, bare,
no hands to tend,
no love to share.

A symbol of neglect,
of decay,
a testament to time
slowly fading away.

In quiet suffering,
a story holds
of love forgotten
and dreams grown cold.
Even in darkness,
there's beauty to find
in neglected corners
of our mind.

Despondent

In shadows deep, where silence reigns,
a heart beats alone, echoing pains.
No warmth to touch, no gentle caress;
just emptiness lingering, a soul's distress.

In the garden of hearts, mine stands bare,
neglected by love in the cold, harsh air.
No blossoms bloom, no sweet scent to find;
just thorns of neglect piercing the mind.

I whisper to the stars, my silent plea,
but they turn away, refusing to see.
In the vast expanse of this lonely night,
I'm a lost soul consumed by blight.

Echoes of laughter, distant and faint,
mocking reminders of love's cruel taint.
I reach out in darkness, grasping at air,
finding only solitude, my constant despair.

Ignored by affection, shunned by care,
I wander aimlessly, lost in despair.
No refuge in sight, no solace to borrow;
just the weight of sorrow, drowning in sorrow.

Alone in this world, forgotten and forsaken,
a heartache so deep it feels like it's taken.
But still, I cling to hope, a flicker so small,
praying to God to answer my call.

Here I remain, in the depths of despair,
hoping against hope that someone will care.
For even in darkness, a glimmer may start
to finally fill this lonely heart.

To Re-emerge

Through the tears that fall,
I find my way,
Gathering strength with each new day.
Though battered and bruised,
I rise once more,
Ready to face what lies in store.

In the wreckage of love,
I search for light
To guide me through the endless night.

No longer defined by the pain I've known,
I'll build myself up,
brick by stone.
With every step
I reclaim my power,
No longer confined to my darkest hour.

For in the depths of despair,
I find my voice:
a song of resilience,
my ultimate choice.

I look beyond this tired scene—
a flicker of hope,
a yearning for life,
a desire to cope.

Even in the deepest frost,
a root may stir and grow
Cracking the silence where sorrows flow.
For with a gentle touch
and a heart sincere,
We can resurrect joy
and banish despair.

Withered blooms lament.
Heart echoes in solitude.
Hope flickers unseen.

Part 4 - The Vase in Need of a Cleanse

There comes a moment in everyone's life when the familiar rhythm of our lives feels more like a monotonous hum than a vibrant symphony. It's a stage where the air is heavy with the scent of stagnation, and the soul longs for a fresh breeze to sweep away the cobwebs of routine. This is the time for a soulful spring clean, a shedding of old skins and a welcoming of new beginnings.

Picture yourself standing at the threshold of possibility, with the weight of inertia pulling at your ankles. It's as if you're encased in amber, frozen in a state of comfortable numbness. But deep within, there's a restless stirring, a yearning for change that whispers in the silence of your heart.

Shaking things up at this life stage is akin to stepping into a cluttered room and deciding to rearrange the furniture. It's about daring to disrupt the status quo, to challenge the boundaries of your comfort zone, and to invite the unfamiliar into your midst. Perhaps it's quitting a job that no longer fulfils you, or finally embarking on that passion project you've been putting off for years.

It's about embracing the discomfort of uncertainty, knowing that growth often sprouts from the fertile soil of discomfort. Just as the caterpillar must dissolve into mush within its cocoon before emerging as a butterfly, so too must we surrender to the transformative power of change.

In this stage of life, shaking things up may manifest as traveling to a foreign land, immersing yourself in a different culture to gain fresh perspectives. It could be delving into spiritual practices such as reconnecting with God. Or perhaps it's as simple as having a heart-to-heart conversation with a loved one, laying bare your vulnerabilities in pursuit of deeper intimacy.

Whatever form it takes, the essence of it lies in you reclaiming your agency, in realising that you are the author of your own narrative. It's about infusing your life with intention and purpose, about savouring the bittersweet beauty of impermanence.

The Cleansing

In the corner of a quiet room, a vase stands tall,
Its once-gleaming surface now obscured by time's call;
A vessel of forgotten dreams, of memories past,
Bearing the weight of neglect, its beauty amassed.

Within its depths, stagnant water lies still,
A murky pool where time seems to stand nil,
Gathered with the remnants of wilted flowers gone by,
Their vibrant hues faded, their fragrance a sigh.

But in this silence, a whisper of hope lingers near,
As if the vase itself calls for someone to appear,
With gentle hands and a heart full of grace,
To cleanse away time's marks, to find its rightful place.

So with tender care, the cleaning begins;
As water flows, the restoration wins,
Each stroke a promise of renewal and light,
Washing away the darkness, banishing the night.

With each pass, the water runs clear and bright,
Cleansing the vessel, bringing it back to life,
As if the vase itself breathes a sigh of relief,
Its surface gleaming, its beauty a belief.

And as the last drop falls, a transformation complete,
The vase stands anew, its beauty replete,
No longer burdened by neglect's heavy hand,
But standing proud in its rightful stand.

Now, once again, the vase shines bright,
A symbol of hope, of renewal, of light;
For even in the darkest corners of despair,
A touch of love and care can bring repair.

The Healing

In the quiet ache of a tired heart,
A path unfolds—a chance to restart.
Where pain once lingered, sharp and deep,
Now rises a call from wounds that sleep.

The ache is old, but change is near,
As stillness clears what once was fear.
Not by forgetting, nor by flight,
But walking through the darkest night.

With gentle strength, the soul begins,
To wash away the dirt, to shed old skins.
Each breath a balm, each tear release,
Each step a turning toward inner peace.

Forgiveness whispers, soft but sure,
Not as escape, but as a cure.
The heart, once guarded, slowly yields—
Its walls give way, its truth revealed.

Where bitterness once claimed its place,
Now grows compassion, slow and grace.
And in this shift, the light breaks through,
A pulse renewed, a self made true.

At last, it dances, light and wide,
Unashamed of what it holds inside.
For healing is not just to survive—
But to rise again, fully alive.

The Inviting Soul

With a cleansed heart, an open sky,
I seek to feel, to laugh, to cry.
Every emotion a colour bright,
Painting the canvas of my newfound light.

I want to feel the warmth of the sun,
The gentle breeze when the day is done;
To dance with joy, to sing with glee
And let my heart fly wild and free.

I want to taste the sweetness of love,
Like honey from the skies above,
To feel its warmth, its tender grace,
And let it fill every empty space.

I want to embrace the sting of pain,
To know that loss is not in vain,
For in its depths, I'll find the strength
To rise again, no matter the length.

I want to be filled with wonder and awe,
To marvel at the world I saw,
To feel the pulse of life's heartbeat
In every moment, in every street.

I want to know the depths of sorrow,
To understand what makes us hollow,
And from that darkness, find the light
To guide me through the darkest night.

I want to feel it all, every emotion,
To dive headfirst into life's ocean,
For in its depths, I'll find my truth,
And in its waves, I'll find my youth.

So with a cleansed heart, open wide,
I'll let the emotions be my guide,
For in feeling everything, I'll find
The beauty in this heart of mine.

Cleansed vessel, once lost,
Now gleams with hope's gentle touch;
Renewed, it stands tall.

Part 5 - The Vase of Overcompensation

In the flurry of ambition and the zeal for growth, there exists a pivotal life stage wherein we often find ourselves engulfed in the fervour of overcompensation. It's a time when the pendulum swings too far, when we push the limits, sometimes recklessly, in an attempt to seize every opportunity that presents itself. This stage, akin to a fervent sprint at the starting line, often marks the transition from adolescence to adulthood, or even during midlife crises.

Picture the eager college graduate, adorned with aspirations as vast as the horizon itself. Armed with a freshly-inked degree, they plunge headfirst into the professional world, chasing promotions and accolades with a fervour that knows no bounds. They take on extra projects, work overtime, and sacrifice personal time for the allure of advancement, driven by the fear of falling behind or failing to meet societal expectations. They often reach burnout much too soon and are only moments away from a mental breakdown.

Similarly, consider the newlywed couple, brimming with ardor and determination to create the perfect life together. In their quest for marital bliss, they may rush into major life decisions like buying a house, starting a family, or pursuing demanding careers without fully considering the consequences. The desire to prove their love and commitment often leads them to overextend themselves financially, emotionally, and physically.

Even in the realm of personal development, this stage manifests as a whirlwind of self-improvement efforts. Picture the individual who embarks on a fitness journey with unparalleled gusto, adopting extreme diets and rigorous workout regimens in pursuit of the elusive ideal physique. They may neglect crucial aspects of self-care, such as rest and balanced nutrition, in their relentless pursuit of perfection.

In essence, this life stage is characterised by a sense of urgency, a relentless drive to achieve and excel at any cost. Yet beneath the veneer of productivity and ambition lies a vulnerability—a fear of inadequacy, of being left behind in the race of life. It's a stage where the lines between passion and obsession blur, where the quest for success often comes at the expense of our well-being.

A Precarious State

In a corner, once empty, a vase sat,
Its void reverberating, a silent chasm.
Days and nights passed, longing for a bloom,
Yet solitude persisted in the dim-lit room.

Weeks bled into months, time slipping away;
The vessel remained barren under the sky's sway.
But fate, that capricious force, intervened,
Weaving life's whims into a scene unseen.

One day, hastily, with fervent yearning,
The vase was filled, its past yearning spurning.
Blooms cascaded forth, a riot of hues,
Unaware of the burden they would imbue.

With each added stem, weight accrued;
Top-heavy, precarious, the vessel subdued.
Once empty, now struggling to stand,
Beneath life's weight, too much to command.

Petals entangled, stems interwoven,
The vase trembled, destiny enshrouded.
Tipping and swaying, on the precipice it danced—
A delicate equilibrium, fate's ruthless advance.

Then with a shudder, it all collapsed;
The vase shattered, its dreams entrapped.
In eagerness, it forgot the art
Of moderation's embrace, tearing apart.

So heed this tale, this cautionary decree,
Of moderation's wisdom in every plea.
For a once-vacant vessel now lies fractured,
Its lesson learned, in silence captured.

The Desire of Excess

In the tempest of emotion, tread with care,
For the heart, a tender vessel, can rupture,
Bursting with the weight of joy's exuberance,
Or collapsing beneath the crushing weight of sorrow.

Beware the ecstasy that blinds,
A euphoria so intense it blinds reason,
Seducing with its siren song,
Leading to cliffs of reckless abandon.

Too much happiness, a sweet poison,
Intoxicating, clouding judgment's gaze,
A fire that consumes all in its path,
Leaving only ashes in its wake.

And grief, oh, grief, a relentless tide,
Dragging the soul into the abyss
Where despair's shadows loom
And hope flickers like a dying ember.

To dance on the edge of excitement
Is to court the danger of a precipice
Where euphoria meets madness
And the line between thrill and terror blurs.

So temper the flames of emotion
With the cool waters of reason and restraint,
For in the turbulent sea of feeling
Lies both salvation and peril.

Moderation in Earnest

In the chaos of emotions, we often find
Our hearts overwhelmed in a constant bind.
Joy, sorrow, love, and fear—
A tumultuous storm, always near.

Like a garden untended, emotions run wild
In the quest for happiness, like a desperate child.
But in the frenzy of feeling, we often forget
The balance we need to find solace and reset.

For contentment lies not in the extreme,
But in the gentle rhythm, like a soothing dream.
To feel at peace, to find our way,
We must learn to moderate, come what may.

Like a skilled gardener tends to their plot,
We must nurture our emotions with care and thought.
Weeding out excess, pruning with grace,
Balancing our feelings in life's endless race.

For in moderation, true contentment lies
Beneath the vast, ever-changing skies.
With a heart in balance, we find our place
And in the stillness within, we discover grace.

Blossoms bloom, weight grows,
Heart sways on life's fragile edge—
Moderation's dance.

Part 6 - The Vase of Contentment

In this idyllic life stage, contentment envelops like a warm embrace, where every aspect of existence seems to harmonise effortlessly. Picture a tranquil scene: a serene lakeside nestled amidst verdant hills, the water mirroring the azure sky above, gently rippling in the soft breeze.

In this moment of equilibrium, one finds oneself in sync with the rhythm of life, much like the steady pulse of the earth beneath one's feet. Responsibilities are met with ease, akin to a skilled conductor orchestrating a symphony, each note resonating in perfect harmony. Work becomes a fulfilling pursuit, a passion-driven endeavour rather than a mere obligation, where every task completed feels like a stroke on a masterpiece canvas.

Relationships flourish in this balanced realm, much like a well-tended garden blooming with vibrant colours. Friendships are pillars of support, sturdy and unwavering, while love radiates like the gentle glow of a sunset, casting a warm glow over shared moments and memories.

Health and well-being are cherished treasures, nurtured with care and attention. Nourishing meals feed both body and soul, while exercise becomes a joyful ritual, a celebration of vitality and strength. Sleep comes easily, a restorative balm that rejuvenates and replenishes, preparing one for the adventures that await in the waking hours.

In this perfect balance of contentment, time itself seems to slow, allowing one to savour each precious moment like a sip of rich, aromatic coffee, freshly brewed and steaming in the morning light. With each sip, the complex flavours dance upon the palate, awakening the senses and inviting contemplation.

This life stage, though fleeting, is a reminder of the beauty that lies in embracing the present moment, of finding peace amidst the chaos, and of cherishing the simple pleasures that make life truly extraordinary.

Picture-Perfect

In a room bathed in golden light
Stands a vase, a stunning sight;
Its form a sculpted delight
Holding treasures, colours bright.

Within its porcelain embrace,
A symphony of blooms finds place,
Each petal a stroke of grace
In this harmonious, fragrant space.

Roses crimson, velvet-red;
Tulips tall, their heads outspread;
Lilies white, their fragrance spread—
In the vase, their beauty wed.

With just the perfect measure
Of water, a liquid treasure,
They bloom in radiant leisure,
A scene no words can truly measure.

Each bloom a story to tell,
In this arrangement they dwell;
A kaleidoscope, a spell,
In this vase where dreams swell.

So let this sight remind:
In every corner, beauty we find;
In the heart, in the mind,
In every bloom, life defined.

Fulfilment

A content heart is one that dances with joy,
Like a melody that's sweet, without any cloy;
It's the warmth of the sun, the calm of the sea.
It's the laughter of children, wild and free.

It's the soft sigh of wind through the trees,
The buzzing of bees, the hum of the breeze.
It's the colours of sunset, the stars in the night.
It's the feeling of everything being just right.

A content heart is a garden in bloom
With flowers of happiness, banishing gloom.
It's a symphony playing, a beautiful song.
It's a feeling that carries the soul along.

It's the peace that comes with a quiet mind,
The love that's felt, gentle and kind.
It's gratitude for each moment, each day.
A content heart in every way.

So let joy fill your heart, let it overflow;
Let happiness in, let your spirit glow.
For a content heart is a treasure, it's true,
And it's waiting inside, just for you.

Ungrateful Woes

In the calm of contentment, I find my peace:
A tranquil harbour where all worries cease.
With joy in my heart and a smile on my face,
I bask in the warmth of this serene embrace.

But beware, for contentment can quietly deceive,
Leading one to forget and to disbelieve.
In its gentle embrace, ambition may sleep
While gratitude fades, buried deep.

For contentment, though sweet, can breed neglect,
And in its soft embrace, we may forget
The effort it took to reach this place,
The challenges conquered, the trials we faced.

So let us be grateful, let us be aware;
Contentment is a gift, but we must take care.
To stay attentive, to keep our eyes open wide,
For opportunities beckon, just outside.

Let contentment be a beacon, a guiding light,
But let us not forget to keep our sights
On the dreams we hold and the goals we chase,
For in balance lies true contentment's grace.

Amid blooms, a dance,
Content heart in nature's trance.
Grateful, life's expanse.

Part 7 - The Vase on Stable Ground

In the embrace of stability, one finds oneself firmly rooted in a life stage that exudes reliability and steadfastness. Picture a sturdy oak tree, its mighty branches stretching towards the sky, unwavering against the winds of change. This life stage embodies the essence of resilience and dependability, much like the aged trunk of that oak tree.

In this phase, one's foundations are solid, built upon years of experience, learning, and growth. Like the well-constructed walls of a timeless fortress, there's a sense of security and assurance that comes with knowing oneself and one's capabilities. It's akin to standing on solid ground, feeling the firmness beneath one's feet, and knowing that you can weather any storm that may come one's way.

Professionally, this stage might manifest as an expert in a particular field, someone whose knowledge and expertise are highly valued and sought after. They're the go-to person, the reliable pillar of support upon which others lean for guidance and direction.

Personally, this stability might translate into a settled home life, surrounded by loved ones and cherished memories. It's the comforting familiarity of routines and traditions, the steady rhythm of everyday life that brings a sense of contentment and fulfilment.

In relationships, this stage is characterised by trust and loyalty, where bonds are forged through shared experiences and mutual respect. Much like the enduring bond between old friends, there's a sense of ease and understanding that comes with knowing someone deeply and being known in return.

Overall, this life stage is a sanctuary of reliability and strength, a haven where one can find solace and reassurance amidst the ebb and flow of life's uncertainties.

Solid Ground

In the stillness of the room it stands,
A vessel of grace upon steady lands;
Unshakable, unwavering, strong,
Amidst a world where all seems wrong.

Upon its surface, stories unfold,
Tales of courage, of love untold,
A metaphor for all that's pure
In a world where uncertainty lures.

Its base firmly planted, roots deep and true,
Defying the winds that through life blew
An allegory of resilience and might.
In the darkest hour, a guiding light.

Through storms it stands, unyielding, bold,
A symbol of hope that never grows old.
On firm ground, it will not sway;
A beacon of strength, come what may.

In its stillness, a lesson we find
That true strength comes from the mind;
No matter what trials may befall,
Stand firm, stand tall, through it all.

Assured and Free

In the embrace of love's unyielding might,
I stand, a titan bathed in celestial light.
Confidence courses through every vein;
As assurance shields me from doubt's disdain.

In love's sanctuary, I find my repose:
A fortress where my heart forever knows
That in the arms of my beloved's grace,
I'm fortified against life's fierce embrace.

With every beat, my heart sings a song,
A melody of faith, unwavering and strong.
For in their eyes, I see my reflection clear—
A mirror of support, ever sincere.

Belief becomes a beacon, guiding my way
Through the darkest of nights, to the brightest of days.
With each step forward, I boldly tread,
Knowing their love is my armour, my stead.

In the tapestry of life, woven with care,
Their presence is the thread, beyond compare.
Assurance sprouts like a flower in bloom,
Dispelling shadows and banishing gloom.

Oh, what ecstasy floods my soul's vast expanse
When wrapped in love's arms, in harmonious dance!
Confidence, belief, assurance entwine,
Creating a symphony, divine and sublime.

So let the heavens rejoice, let the stars align,
For in the embrace of love, all fears resign.
Exaggerated? Perhaps, but how could it be?
When love's support elevates me, sets me free.

The Minor Hiccup

Amidst the symphony of love's sweet refrain,
A subtle whisper of doubt begins to gain
A foothold in the chambers of my mind,
A shadow creeping, subtle and unkind.

Though confidence once stood tall and strong,
A seed of suspicion, it doesn't belong.
It gently rocks the boat of my certainty,
Causing ripples in love's tranquil sea.

Belief, once unwavering, now starts to wane
As tiny cracks appear in love's grand domain.
The doubts, like ghosts, begin to haunt,
Casting shadows where there once was no want.

Assurance, once a fortress, now seems frail
As whispers of uncertainty start to assail.
The certainty I held with steadfast trust
Now seems to crumble, turning to dust.

Oh, how quickly the tides of doubt can rise,
Obscuring the truth, veiling the skies.
Yet still, I cling to love's fragile shore,
Hoping the whispers will plague me no more.

But in the depths of my heart, a fear does dwell
That these doubts may grow, and love may quell.
Yet still I hold on, with all my might,
Praying that love's beacon will guide me through the night.

In love's sturdy arms,
Doubt's whispers fade, hearts entwine,
Assurance prevails.

Part 8 - The Vase on Rocky Ground

Whilst life may be stable at times, there are stages where stability seems as elusive as a fleeting shadow. They are times when the ground beneath one's feet feels perpetually shaky, as if one is tiptoeing across a field of jagged rocks, never quite finding solid footing.

Picture a lone traveler navigating a treacherous mountain pass, each step met with the uncertainty of loose gravel and shifting terrain. Every decision feels like a gamble, each choice carrying the weight of potential consequence. It's a period where relationships strain under the pressure of conflicting desires and evolving identities, resembling the jagged edges of fractured stone.

In this tumultuous phase, careers resemble a turbulent sea, with waves of uncertainty crashing against the shores of ambition. Job security becomes a distant dream, as layoffs and restructurings loom like storm clouds on the horizon. Each professional endeavour feels like a delicate balancing act on the precipice of success and failure, mirroring the precariousness of a climber scaling a sheer rock face.

Personal growth, too, takes on a rocky complexion during this life stage. Like a plant struggling to find purchase in barren soil, individuals grapple with self-doubt and existential questioning. Identity crisis becomes a familiar companion as one searches for meaning amidst the chaos of transition and change.

In the end, this tumultuous life stage serves as a crucible, refining individuals through the fires of challenge and adversity. Whilst one may emerge stronger through navigating these uncertain waters, they can leave one shaken to one's core, unable to brace oneself for the fall.

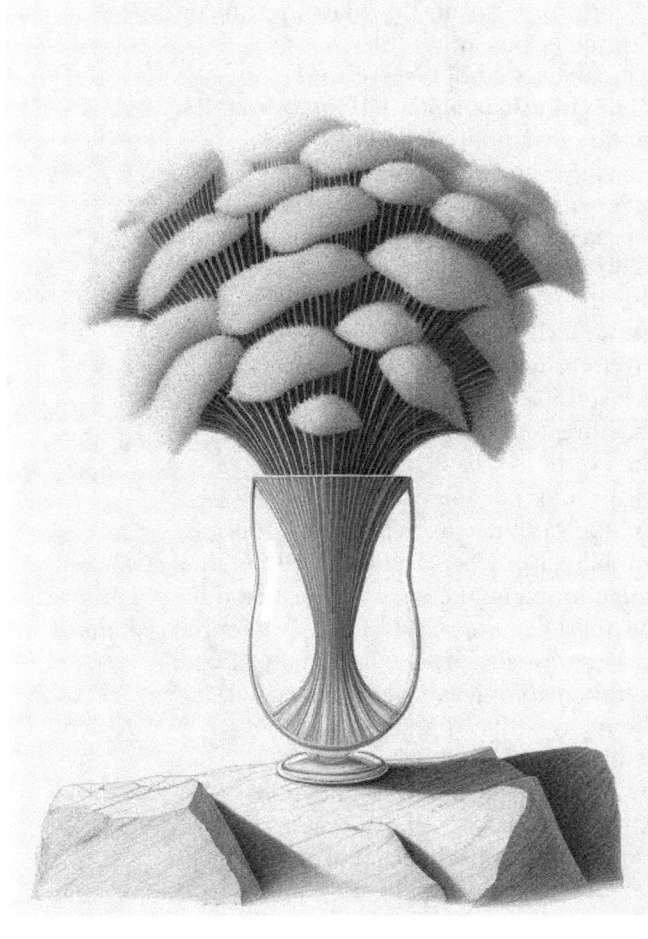

The Unforeseen Knock

Upon the rugged stone it rests,
A vessel crafted by hands unseen;
Smooth curves against the harshness below,
A fragile beauty amidst the chaos.
In its stillness it holds secrets,
Echoes of distant lands and forgotten tales
Captured within its delicate form,
A silent witness to the passage of time.
But the ground beneath is not kind,
Its jagged edges whispering of danger,
A constant threat to the fragile peace
That the vase precariously maintains.
And so it shakes, ever so slightly,
A tremor born of uncertainty,
As if sensing the impending storm,
That threatens to shatter its tranquility.
Then without warning, it happens,
A force unseen, a knock unforeseen,
And the vase succumbs to gravity's call,
Tumbling from its perch with a resounding crash.
In that moment, the silence is shattered,
Fractured like the shards that now litter the ground,
And the vase lies broken, a casualty of fate,
Its story incomplete, its beauty marred.
The rocky surface remains unmoved,
A silent witness to the dance of fate.
For even the sturdiest of foundations
Can be shaken by the unforeseen,
And even the most delicate of vessels
Can be broken by the slightest touch.

Jolted and Rattled

In the quiet moments,
When the world feels steady,
And emotions rest like stones in a riverbed,
There comes a quake,
A seismic shift in the soul.
It arrives unannounced,
A tempest within,
Sweeping away certainties,
Leaving only the raw edge
Of disbelief and upheaval.
We thought we knew,
Built castles of belief
On the sands of our understanding,
Yet here we stand,
Waves crashing at our foundations.
Emotions, once familiar,
Now surge like untamed rivers,
Rushing through the canyons of our being,
Carrying us to uncharted territories
Of vulnerability and doubt.
What we once believed was solid
Now wavers like shadows in candlelight,
As the unforeseen event
Unfolds its truth before us,
Leaving us breathless,
Reaching for stability in the chaos.
In the aftermath,
We are left reeling,
Grappling with the fragments
Of what we thought was real,
Struggling to rebuild
Amidst the wreckage of our emotions.

The Fall, The Pieces

In the aftermath,
We find ourselves
Amongst the debris of shattered dreams,
Pieces of our once-whole selves
Scattered like forgotten echoes
In the silence of our souls.
What once seemed unbreakable
Now lies fractured,
Each fissure a testament
To the force of unforeseen events,
A reminder of our fragility
In the face of life's capriciousness.
We feel the weight of loss,
Not just of what was,
But of the trust we placed
In the stability of our emotions,
Now revealed as fragile illusions
In the harsh light of reality.
Grief washes over us,
A relentless tide,
Dragging us into depths
Where pain and sorrow intertwine
And we struggle to find
A foothold in the darkness.

Amidst silent stones,
Quakes fracture delicate peace—
Echoes of chaos.

Part 9 - The Shattered Vase

In the dimly-lit room, the cracked plaster on the walls betrays years of neglect, mirroring the fractured state of the occupant's mind. A once-cozy armchair now sits torn and tattered, its upholstery worn thin by the weight of countless sleepless nights and silent tears. The remnants of shattered pottery lay strewn across the floor, a poignant reminder of the violent outbursts that have become all too frequent.

On the coffee table, a stack of unpaid bills forms a disorganised pile, each envelope a harbinger of financial ruin and mounting debt. The telephone, once a lifeline to the outside world, now sits ominously silent, its cord tangled and frayed beyond repair. In the corner, a neglected guitar leans against the wall, its strings broken and its melody silenced, a symbol of abandoned passions and unfulfilled dreams.

Outside the window, the world continues to spin, oblivious to the turmoil within. The distant sounds of laughter and chatter serve only to highlight the oppressive silence that pervades this desolate space. In the kitchen, the remnants of a failed meal sit congealing on the stove, a stark reminder of the futility of even the most mundane tasks.

In the bedroom, the once-cozy bed now lies unmade, its sheets stained with the remnants of fitful sleep and restless nightmares. The closet door hangs askew on its hinges, revealing a jumble of clothes that no longer hold any appeal. Among them, a forgotten suit hangs limply, a relic of a time when success seemed within reach.

This is a life stage where everything has fallen apart, where broken relationships and shattered dreams lay strewn across the landscape like a wreckage after a storm. At times we try to pick up those shattered pieces, seeking redemption, trying to find meaning amidst the chaos in an attempt at rebuilding what was lost.

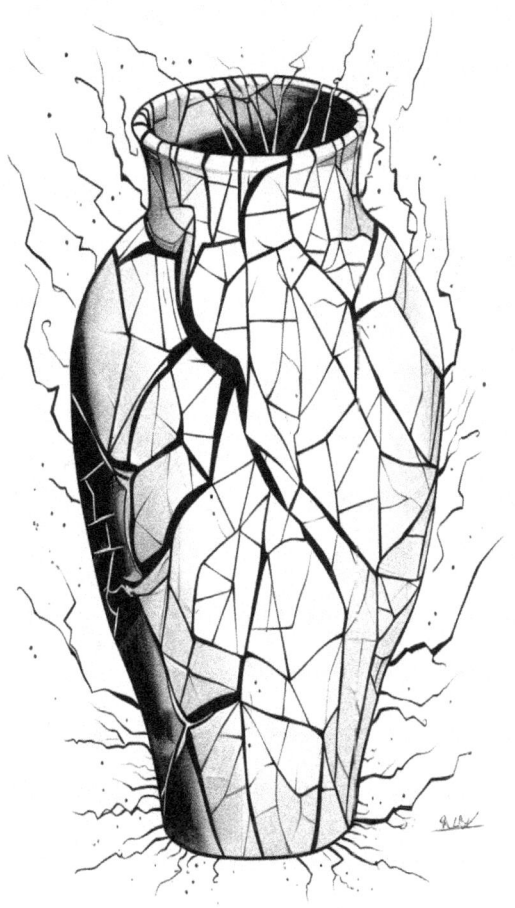

The Shattered Vase

In the dim morning light,
a vase lies shattered,
its porcelain shards spread like fallen stars
across the hardwood floor,
each piece a silent echo of what once held beauty.

Yesterday it stood tall—
a keeper of memories,
holding fresh blooms, a whisper of spring,
a token of fragile hope,
its curves embracing moments and seasons.

Now it's broken beyond repair,
a constellation of jagged edges,
each fragment reflecting a ghost of past tenderness,
a kaleidoscope of grief and silent screams.

I kneel beside the remnants,
fingers trembling as they trace the fault lines,
feeling the sting of loss
in each cruel shard,
the cold, sharp truth of it
cutting deeper than any wound.

The flowers, too, lie scattered,
their petals bruised, wilted,
a muted chorus of sorrow,
their scent mingling with the dust,
a requiem for what can never be restored.

There was a time when this vase was whole,
when it held dreams in its delicate embrace;
but now it speaks only of endings,
of the fragile nature of all things cherished,
of how beauty can be so easily shattered.

I gather the pieces,
though I know they cannot be mended,
each one a reminder
that some losses are final,
that some things, once broken,
remain forever fractured.

The sun rises higher,
casting long shadows on the floor,
and I sit in the stillness,
the weight of absence pressing heavy
as the morning moves on without mercy,
leaving behind only the silence
and the shards of a vase
that once held more than flowers.

The Broken Heart

I sit, shattered
in a mosaic of broken dreams,
tormented by those jagged edges.

The whispers of promises once golden,
now tarnished with betrayal,
echo in the hollow chambers of my heart,
each word a dagger, each lie a wound.

We wove our days with threads of hope,
believing in the strength of us,
but you unraveled the tapestry,
left me clutching frayed edges of what was.

Your eyes, once a sanctuary,
are now cold, distant mirrors reflecting my despair.
I search for warmth, for solace,
and find only the ghost of what we used to be.

There was a time when love was my compass,
guiding me through the dark,
but now I am lost,
adrift in an ocean of sorrow.

I remember the weight of your touch,
the way it anchored me to something real;
now it is a phantom caress,
a cruel reminder of all I've lost.

The world moves on, indifferent,
as I sit among the ruins of our love,
a broken statue, lifeless and still,
praying for the sweet release of forgetting.

In this landscape of grief,
hope is a distant star,
fading and flickering,
as I trace the scars you left behind.

I am a vessel emptied,
a heart hollowed out by your betrayal,
left to gather dust—
a relic of love's cruel deception.

In the silence, I whisper your name,
a prayer, a curse, a lament,
for the heart you shattered,
for the soul you abandoned.

May you know the weight of my sorrow;
may you feel the chill of my despair,
for in your wake, I am but a shadow,
a broken echo of who I once was.

Picking up the Pieces

In the labyrinth of despair, I tread softly,
Heart shattered, fractured into countless pieces,
Each step a hesitant shuffle
Through the fog of grief I seek.

What is this elusive flicker I chase?
A glimmer, a whisper, a faint echo of hope,
Elusive, yet persistent in its dance.
In the crevices of my brokenness,
I reach, fingers trembling, for its touch.

Amidst the chaos of my shattered heart,
I question the fragments strewn before me,
Each shard a puzzle, a piece of the whole,
A riddle waiting to be deciphered.

Through the jagged edges of my despair,
I ponder the meaning of resilience,
A whisper of possibility, a promise of strength,
Lurking in the shadows of my doubt.

In the silence that envelops me,
I question the emptiness that surrounds,
A void waiting to be filled,
A canvas longing for colour, for life.

With each breath, I gather courage,
Asking, searching, seeking;
For in the process of questioning,
I find the seeds of transformation.

In shattered silence,
fragments whisper tales of loss;
hope blooms in rubble.

Part 10 - The Vase of One Thousand Scars

Imagine a woman sitting at her kitchen table, surrounded by fragments of a ceramic bowl—a cherished heirloom shattered in a moment of carelessness. Instead of despair, she sees an opportunity for transformation inspired by the Japanese art of Kintsugi. With gentle hands, she meticulously reassembles the broken pieces, filling the cracks with liquid gold. As she works, she reflects on her own life—a journey marked by trials and tribulations, but also by moments of profound growth and resilience.

Each crack in the bowl becomes a symbol of her own struggles—a failed marriage, a career setback, the loss of a loved one. Yet as she applies the gold lacquer, she realises that these moments of brokenness have not diminished her worth but have made her stronger and more beautiful. Just as the repaired bowl will hold more significance than before, she embraces her scars as reminders of her capacity to endure and thrive.

Elsewhere, in a small workshop, a craftsman meticulously restores a centuries-old painting damaged by time and neglect. As he carefully repairs the torn canvas and faded pigments, he is reminded of his own journey—a childhood marked by poverty and hardship, but also by moments of profound creativity and resilience. Like the Kintsugi artist, he sees beauty in imperfection, and through his work, he seeks to honour the stories embedded in every brushstroke and crack.

In both cases, the act of picking up the pieces and repairing what's broken is not merely a physical task but a deeply emotional and spiritual one. It is a journey of self-discovery and healing—a recognition that our scars do not define us but serve as reminders of our strength and resilience. As the morning sun casts its warm glow, illuminating the repaired bowl and restored painting, it is a testament to the transformative power of embracing our imperfections and treasuring the scars that make us who we are. It is one embraced with our hearts wide open towards the Divine.

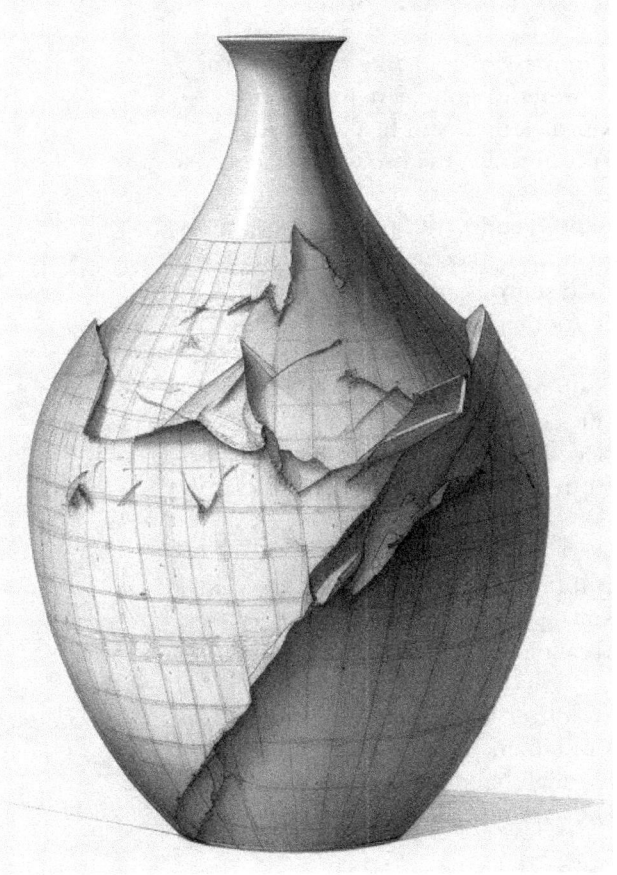

The Mending

Forgotten and abandoned, the vase lies shattered—
Scattered pieces, dreams left tattered.
Once whole, now fragments on the floor,
Echoes of beauty, whispers of more.

Glimmers of gold, like rays of dawn,
Whisper of hope, a new day born.
Kintsugi, the art of healing scars,
Transforming the broken, reaching stars.

Hands gentle, with patience and care,
Gather the pieces, repair to dare.
Each shard is a story, a tale to tell
Of moments lived, of times that fell.

Resin mixed with powdered gold,
Lines of light, a story told.
Piece by piece, the vase reborn
From fragments, a new form adorn.

Every crack a mark of grace,
Embracing flaws, the golden trace.
Kintsugi weaves its magic true,
Creating beauty from what's askew.

No longer broken but uniquely whole,
A testament to the resilient soul.
Through hands of love, the mending done,
The vase now gleams, kissed by the sun.

Lessons learned in every line;
From brokenness, the heart refines.
In golden seams, strength we find,
Healing the vase, healing the mind.

Shattered no more but stronger still;
With every scar, a testament to will.
In Kintsugi's art we see the light
Turning wounds into wings for flight.

Now the vase stands tall and proud,
A symbol of hope to which we're vowed.
In every crack a golden gleam,
In every mend a renewed dream.

The Mended Heart

In the realm of shattered dreams where hearts lay broken,
Amidst the fragments, whispers of words unspoken—
Therein lies a journey, though fraught with pain,
To weave the threads of hope, to dance in the rain.

Step by step, we gather the shards,
Each piece a memory, each cut a bard,
A symphony of sorrow, a melody of woe.
Yet within this chaos, resilience does grow.

With trembling hands and a steadfast will,
We mend the rifts, each crack we fill;
For in the art of healing, there's strength untold,
A courage to rise, a spirit bold.

Through sleepless nights and endless tears,
We confront our fears,
Facing the demons that haunt our soul,
Embracing the pain to finally feel whole.

It's not a journey for the faint of heart,
But a testament to the power to restart,
To rebuild, to rise, to soar above,
Transforming pain into an anthem of love.

With time as our ally and faith as our guide,
We navigate the darkness with hope at our side,
For every scar, a story of survival,
A testament to our unyielding revival.

So let the broken pieces pave our way,
For in the end, we'll emerge, come what may,
With hearts renewed and spirits bright.
We'll conquer the shadows and embrace the light.

For in the monument of life, amidst the art,
There's beauty in the journey of mending a shattered
heart.

The Renewal

I stand, toes curling in fresh dew,
a whisper of uncertainty lingering,
yet a spark of anticipation ignites within.

I carry the weight of past trials,
like pebbles in my pockets,
each one a story etched into my skin,
a roadmap of resilience, of growth.

Through the dark alleys of doubt,
I've stumbled, tripped, and fallen,
but in the depths of my despair,
I discovered the strength to rise again.

For every shattered dream,
I've woven a tapestry of hope,
each thread a testament to my tenacity,
each knot a symbol of my unyielding spirit.

So here in this moment,
I embrace the unknown
with open arms and a fearless heart,
knowing that within every challenge lies opportunity.

With each breath, I affirm:
I am forged by the fires of adversity,
I am shaped by the storms I've weathered,
and with each new beginning,
I am reborn, resilient, and ready to thrive.

Shattered dreams reborn,
Golden threads weave tales untold,
Heart's resilience shown.

Conclusion

Life can be likened to a delicate vase — not merely an object, but a symbol of our capacity to hold, to break and to begin again. That entails the beauty of a vase, a vessel of want and need longing to be filled. As we traverse life, we may find ourselves at any one of these stages. The beauty lies in the fact that there is always a way forward, though it may be harder to push through. We may need more emotion and perseverance than we originally thought, but we will survive.

Those moments when our hearts feel empty and vacant, filled with utter disregard for ourself, can be mended. Just like a vacant vase, we can choose to fill it with blooms of our choosing. We can become more fulfilled and complete if we choose to take a chance and start anew.

The moments when we feel trapped, with the monotony of life dragging us down, can be changed. We can throw out the old water and flowers in the vase. We can relinquish the control that negativity and self-doubt have over us and take a chance on something that may inspire us anew.

Don't forget that the moments of complete elation and perfection, where nothing seems to go wrong, can also set us up for failure. We become accustomed to things always going our way, refusing to change and innovate. A vase filled with the perfect blooms can become stagnant and boring if the water and flowers aren't refreshed.

Thus, nothing in life is perfect. A sudden, unexpected event can shock us to the core, altering our entire trajectory. It can shatter our world, breaking us into pieces, just like a vase placed in harm's way. The key, though, is to persevere and push forward, gluing our shards back together. Those shattered pieces will fashion something new. You can be the embodiment of Kintsugi, a singular masterpiece more valuable with your scars than without them.

So choose to fill your vase wisely, reflecting on your desires, beliefs, and intentions. Be mindful of the Divine, weighing possibilities and consequences, and know that the unexpected can happen, but that, too, can be a process to build upon fashioning something anew.

Empty vase, heart void;
Seeking solace, blooms unfold.
Perseverance fuels.